My String of Pearls

Gems of Wisdom from Awesome Oysters

Jo Anne French

MY STRING OF PEARLS
Gems of Wisdom from Awesome Oysters
by Jo Anne French

Published by:
RPJ LEGACY BOOKS
An Imprint of RPJ & Company, Inc.
Orlando, Florida, U.S.A.
Web site: www.rpjandco.com | www.rpjandco1417.com

ISBN-13: 978-1-937770-56-3
ISBN-10: 1-937770-56-7

Cover Image:
Pearl Necklace © Sommai Damrongpanich / 123RF

Background Effect:
Alex and Griffin Kinkade, grandsons of the author

Interior Pearl Border:
Elegant frame of pearls © Tatiana Prikhnenko / 123RF

Interior Clam Image:
Shiny pearl in opened seashell © mikado767 / 123RF

Cover and Interior Design Consultant:
Kathleen Schubitz | www.rpjandco1417.com

Printed in the United States of America

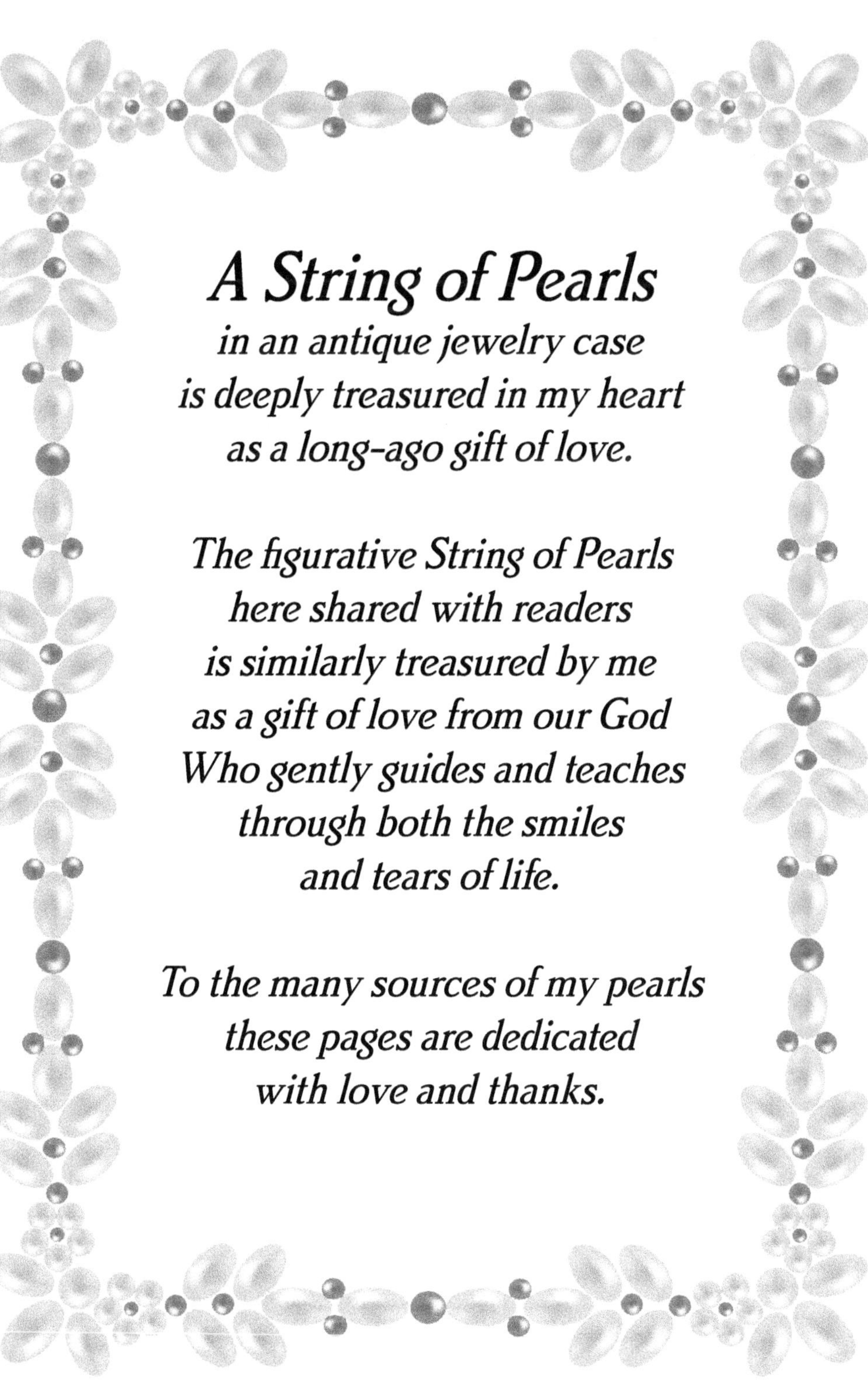

A String of Pearls

in an antique jewelry case
is deeply treasured in my heart
as a long-ago gift of love.

The figurative String of Pearls
here shared with readers
is similarly treasured by me
as a gift of love from our God
Who gently guides and teaches
through both the smiles
and tears of life.

To the many sources of my pearls
these pages are dedicated
with love and thanks.

My String of Pearls

Finding My Pearls

Finding More Pearls

My String of Pearls

is an engaging memory album
of life-affirming insights
and must-share stories.

Some are tales of smiles and fun;
a few have sadness and challenge.
Playful analogy throughout
introduces an array of strange
but helpful oysters who came
bearing gems of wisdom,
now shared with my readers.

Enjoy!

11

Master Puzzle Maker

A JIGSAW was among tools on the workbench of my Father and Grandfather before most people even knew what it was, or what intriguing puzzles it could create.

Jigsaw puzzles were a favorite childhood pastime of mine, perhaps mostly because it was so special that adults would spend that kind of patient time with me. My Grandfather was unable to walk in his last years, so he asked for a small table by the bed in his room in order for him to supervise his granddaughter in this pursuit. Many memorable ones were tackled, but the best were the ones he and my Father had made.

We still have a few of these among family treasures. Our very favorite is a large one we call the Scarecrow Puzzle. It is a grizzled corn farmer lurking behind his scarecrow with rifle in hand, waiting for the offending birds.

This puzzle, we have deduced, reveals devious humor of the men who made it. In a couple places, such as along the rifle, there are straight edges like those usually found only around the outer rim. And along the outer rim are pieces which come to a point rather than having the expected straight edge. So much for that routine sorting of pieces to proceed efficiently with putting the picture together!

In times of personal dilemma in my life, these puzzle memories present new perspectives. Some pieces just do not fit where it seems they should go. Or some parts of my life take shape in ways that do not conform to my own plans or assumptions. But a Master Puzzle Maker is at work. He knows where all the pieces belong, and sees the completed picture before it is clear to me.

My pearl gathered here from the jigsaw oyster: *Trust that Master. He will create a meaningful picture out of my jumble of puzzle pieces!*

No Fair Peeking

MY MOTHER'S SECRET stashing place for gifts, often handmade by her, was well known to me in my childhood years. Two things were true: the inviting temptation, and the diminished delight at present opening time. In more mature years, something such as a sneak peek at a sales slip or credit card bill might reveal a planned surprise from my husband. Oh, such big mistakes!

My pearl here from this generous oyster: *Respect that intended surprise! Then there is added pleasure for both giver and receiver.*

Lost in the Revolving Door

DOWNTOWN SEATTLE was always a treat, no matter what errands of my Mother or older sisters took us there. It may or may not directly involve me… such as photographs or shopping for clothes…it just made me feel grown up to be included in the trip.

One particular day while my older sister was waiting in line at a bank, my wandering eyes analyzed the side door. Even my tiny-girl arms could handle that… just shove a bit and it went through sort of a circular place. Asking my sister's permission first, checking that out seemed a necessary task. Sure enough, my gentle push was all it took to get me outside all by myself. *Okay, now what?*

The sidewalk looked sort of familiar. That traffic light up to the right was where we had just crossed the street. No one was around to tell me for sure, but it seemed definite to me that the bank's front door was just around the corner. Heading there to enter the way we had before seemed the only answer.

Rejoining my still-waiting sister in her line, she was mystified by my dazed look together with the fact that my entry had just been through the front door. "But you could have gotten lost," she chided. "All you needed to do was keep pushing and let the door go in its circle and bring you back in right there."

In my defense it should be noted that reading and writing came for me in very early years, and top grades throughout school and college followed. Despite what should have been adequate brain power, revolving doors simply had not entered my experience as yet.

The pearl added to my string from the revolving door oyster colored my mind through years of rearing sons, and many other encounters: *What is crystal clear or even laughingly obvious to me may be entirely new experience for someone else, youngster or otherwise. Be accordingly patient!*

Two Wrongs, No Right

A GUM PACK went into my pocket, in one of those utterly unexplained childhood transgressions. Only a few steps away my know-better conscience got to me. As the pack was then opened, my only option was to repay the five cents. What to say? How to explain? Finally in desperation, my five pennies were quietly left on a shelf away from the grocer's view. But my disciplining oyster later taught me: *Taking in secret was wrong and repaying in secret equally wrong. It is so much better to confess the indiscretion!*

Just a Hole in the Wall

"HOLE IN THE WALL" often describes a favorite small shopping place or out-of-the-way restaurant. This one recalls an embarrassing childish tantrum. My naptime on our upstairs sleeping porch was over, and it was time to loudly summon my Mother. She did not come right away and for some reason it seemed necessary for me to bang the door back against the wall again and again to punctuate my distress. After a gentle bottom-swat from my usually very patient Mother, she pointed out the significant hole created in the wall behind the door.

In all my growing up years my Father did not repair that hole though he surely had materials and tools to do so. He had after all built our home, and improved and maintained it continually for a couple decades. It can only be guessed, but perhaps he was leaving an unspoken lesson for me.

My sister continued to live next door to our childhood home, so there was opportunity well into my adulthood to visit again. It was impossible to know whether to laugh or cry upon finding that *the hole in the wall was still there;* multiple new owners had not fixed it either in over 40 years.

From this unplastered oyster, a pearl of wisdom was added to my string:

Whether from adults or from a child's fairly innocent realm, permanent or embarrassing results do grow from thoughtless acts.

PS conjecture. What can repair or correct those results? Communication, sharing, forgiveness? Or perhaps we need more patient perception to keep those "holes" from happening in the first place!

I remember…and lean in longing
toward the house wherein I grew.
Kahlil Gibran, A Tear and a Smile

In the Garden

FAITH OF MY ANCESTORS shines in many word pictures encountered in family research. Despite fervent practices and strong testimony in prior generations, it was true that for years my Father let employment schedules prevail over his own church attendance…while he did still encourage my siblings and me to follow the old paths.

My Father's favorite hymn, "I Come to the Garden Alone" is hummed by this oyster with his reminder: *Be thankful for roadways of faith which came strongly over an up-and-down path, then strive to level that path for more family yet ahead!*

A Yellowstone Pearl

STRANGERS' TEARFUL SEPARATION a lifetime ago, between my fourth and fifth grade year, forever colored my life.

My family was at Yellowstone Park, taking every possible tour of every possible attraction. My newly-acquired box camera was being frequently tested. One evening it seemed a pleasant time, with permission, to wander just a bit and perhaps take a few more pictures near our cabin. From another cabin fairly close by came the sound of loud voices, shouting and screaming. Before long a raging man came storming out. He tossed a few things into the back seat and sped away in an old automobile, leaving a hysterical wife at the doorstep.

This was all so confusing to me, for throughout my life such things just had not occurred. Never was my Mother known to raise her voice in anger, despite much provocation from an active family. My Father was not nearly so patient, but shouting was just not his way of family communication. So what was this all about? What could it mean? The bio of my nine-year-old life simply did not include experience needed to help weigh or understand.

After a quick meal with my family, a troubling and perhaps morbid curiosity drew me once more to the cabin where that violent argument had occurred. It was darkened. The automobile was still gone. Walking nearby, what greeted me this time was doleful sobbing from within. If only it were possible for a big hug from a young passerby to ease her pain! With no adult understanding of it all, my too-young mind was still very deeply touched.

That Yellowstone couple may or may not have ever gotten back together. Nevertheless they gave me valuable…and scary…insights not shared with anyone for years. Their intense arguing and that woman's sobbing gave me the firmest determination that no such thing would ever happen to me. Separations came, sadly yes, but very much minus the rancor. The pearl from my Yellowstone oyster reminds me: *Angry words can tear lives apart. Love is the only healing answer!*

If you are patient in one moment of anger
you will save a thousand days of sorrow.
Chinese Proverb

When they walk through the Valley of Weeping,
it will become a place of refreshing springs
where pools of blessing collect after the rains!
Psalm 84:6 NLT

Where's the Beef?

PICNIC. Just the word generally conjures smiling recollections and happy thoughts. However, my most memorable one had a few odd turns embarrassingly caused mostly by me…starting with a haunting *where's the beef?* moment.

This special day was not particularly sunny, but that seemed not to matter as our junior choir members headed for a Mount Rainier park with cookout fun in mind. A friend had come for a sleepover at my home. It had been our responsibility to purchase, pack and transport the ground beef for our hamburger lunch, along with a few favorite accompaniments. Others promised chips, drinks, dessert and such.

Imagine our consternation as we began organizing for lunch. "Where's the beef?" someone asked. Where indeed? Home in our freezer, it was finally concluded. "Well, there is more food here. We will be okay."

Among many giggles onion sandwiches emerged, with a little lettuce and tomato disguising the gaping lack. Soon we found our baked beans were unavailable, for the can opener was somewhere near the beef patties at home. A neighboring camper loaned us one and we proceeded as best we could, even with no suitable pot in which to heat the beans.

Oh, and there was watermelon, always a favored treat. Where was the large knife needed to cut that? Another item was borrowed from the helpful campers next to us.

In my growing up years there must have been scores upon scores of picnic experiences, with a huge kaleidoscope of things somehow only stacked next to the memory album but not mounted therein. Which is the picnic most remembered by me? Onion and lettuce sandwiches, barely warm baked beans from a can, roughly cut watermelon wedges, gray skies.

Good fun with friends is special, and those *people* are always more important than the *things.* Defined much later to be sure, a good reminder pearl was added by a vegetarian oyster that day: *Memorable or significant times do not require all parts going on perfect plan...especially with friends present!*

PS: It should be mentioned that packing for any outing throughout the rest of my life has been much more successful. Mistakes do help us learn!

You can make many plans
but the Lord's purpose will prevail.
Proverbs 19:21 NLT

Loads of Room!

WE WERE ON OUR WAY to a late afternoon campfire outing at a lake near Seattle. There were eight or nine of us, our count matching our ages. The driver had checked with the Washington State Patrol to be sure of rules. She was advised that there should be no more than three in the front seat, including her. If the rest of us could cram into the back for the short drive planned, all would be well.

Somewhere near our campsite, flashing lights loomed. But we had asked! Could they possibly arrest us for a crowded back seat? My friend's shouted imperative and the picture it evokes still bring laughter after all these decades. To the six of us wedged between or on each other's laps in the back seat she firmly directed, grammar glitch and all, "Quick! Sit like there is loads of room!"

That made no difference of course, for the problem actually was a U-turn, and failure to yield right of way upon re-entering traffic. The patrolman gave firm admonishment about that detail, smiled at us girls crowded in the back seat and waved us on our way.

Fear most often is based on unknown or incomplete facts. No time should be wasted in worry about what may never even come to pass. My pearl from a very scrunched-up oyster: *Just act in faith, relax, and "Sit like there is loads of room!"*

22

Hike More Often?

SOME PROFOUND WISDOM is just handed to us, literally. Special insight from my Mother showed me that our best life lessons need not come through a begrudging, "My parents were *always* telling me about that" kind of scenario.

Recalled here are wise words my Mother said to me *one* time, and yes, shared often and remembered continually along both smooth and rocky pathways. For a long while they aided in my discipline of biking at least ten miles daily though much pain was involved as knee surgery loomed. This is the principle: if it hurts a little, or if it is a challenge, then just work on it until it gets easier.

My Mother's actual memorable words expressing this came framed in an unlikely picture…or call this the unlikely oyster on our hiking trail. It produced one of the most treasured pearls for my string on the day after a young people's group had gone on a mountain hike. That was an endeavor not at all familiar to me, and it seemed my pain and soreness were going to last forever. Tending to physical aid and comfort measures, my Mother quietly asked,

"What have you been doing that you should not do?" She added her zinger with the thinnest trace of a smile: *"…or that you should do more often?"*

Finding the Prophet

IN BACK STACKS OF THE LIBRARY at Whitworth University my searching produced an array of sources for current studies. Rather hidden on one dusty shelf, a copy of Kahlil Gibran's *The Prophet* appeared. A quick leafing through seemed to promise me more enticing reading than the others garnered.

It was indeed so. Psalms of David and the Proverbs of Solomon keep easy company with the profound insights of Gibran. Untouched on the library table, my other selected books waited while the astounding work of this matchless Lebanese writer led me on new paths.

Sharing my great find with a tableful of friends at dinner that evening, only an embarrassing feeling of inadequate reading habits resulted. "Did you just find that? Oh, good grief, *everyone* has read his books." Then they all proceeded to share favorite quotations from Gibran and discuss his philosophies.

How had my reading lagged so far behind? It had included comparative world religion theses, Elizabethan and Italian Renaissance writings, the Shakespeare authorship controversy, New Testament Greek guides, Chaucer's medieval works and a wealth of other erudite volumes. These had all found their way from the library to my dorm room, or to those back study desks. But somehow my friends' comments made me feel so uneducated.

From this bookworm oyster, the pearl added to my string that day reminded me: *Actions or words to others should always share or agree rather than belittle, if their experience does not match mine.*

You are as flowers that grow in the shade.
Gentle breezes...bear your needs to the sunlight.
Kahlil Gibran, A Tear and a Smile

The deeper that sorrow carves into your being,
the more joy you can contain.
Kahlil Gibran, The Prophet

Choosing a Cross Road

AN INVERTED DRAWING in our college paper, though an errant view of our printer, still brought a teachable moment. For each issue we prepared inspirational or scriptural thought, appearing with an illustration of a crossroad sign whose shadow formed a cross. It was one time turned over in error, but somehow the message seemed the same. My printshop oyster left this memorable pearl for me: *At any crossroad, choose the Cross road.*

25

OPM with Silver Spoons

ECONOMISTS SPEAK OF OPM...strategies using other people's money. The principle shared here may also be termed OPM...other people's mistakes.

A simple job of making cupcakes turned into minor kitchen catastrophe. One of my good silver spoons got badly mangled within some equally distressed beaters. The instant it happened two things were crystal clear to me: (1) Oh, *that* is why Mother told me never to use a silver spoon in the mixer bowl. And (2) surely she had this happen to her and that is why she knew!

There were years in which Mother did not have much option, for wooden spoons are equally incompatible with beaters. And dictates of the war years meant that rubber was in far flung places of the world, but not in our kitchen. We children came later to prefer the no-scraper years because bowls were more inviting for that "licking" task which followed! Yet Mother had definitely learned it was best not to use silver for the mixer bowls...and she did *try* to pass that tip on to me.

Actually learning the lesson came so much later for me. The pearl for my string that day from the careful baking oyster was not about the wisdom of learning from my mistakes, but about OPM: *How much wiser it is to learn also from other people's mistakes!*

26
Bruce's Peas

CAFETERIA DUTY was not exactly my favorite part of a school day, but even from such mundane things both students and the teacher have much to learn.

What the kids called Clean Plate Club was not at all my policy in this task. Before excusing a group to go on out for their noon break, their lunches… or what remained…were checked to be sure that at least a portion of each menu item was eaten. It was *verboten* to eat just the Jello and cookie while leaving vegetables untouched.

Bruce, one of my brightest students, sat with his lunch suitably consumed while the serving of green peas was fully intact. After my reminder to him, he retorted, "Ugh! Peas are terrible. I cannot stand them."

My suggestion for just a couple bites brought an apparent negative answer, as he continued to rant about the peas. He was not going to have them that day or the next. In fact he had never had them a single time in his life.

Oops. Then he knew he had said the wrong thing. "Bruce, you are so sharp in every other way. How in the world do you know you do not like peas if you have never eaten them before?"

Another student caught my attention and it was time for me to move on. After checking and excusing a couple other tables, my path took me back to Bruce's table. His tray was empty and his smile was big. "You were right! Those peas were really good, and I ate them all!"

It is time to turn this around and teach the teacher the same lesson! When some menu items are avoided with mumbled excuse about not liking them, "never had them before" may be more truthful. Recalling Bruce, my efforts to expand food choices do get tried out from time to time.

Solomon noted that he who answers a matter before hearing it is foolish. That does seem to relate to disliking food before tasting it. My pearl from this lunchroom oyster (one of *those* foods, by the way): *Just try it! New special treats may be added to my life.*

David's Choice

DAVID FACED GOLIATH with very clear choice. "He is so big, running will bring my only safety," OR "He is so big, how can I possibly miss?" My slingshot oyster says: *With God's strength and guidance choosing a positive view is always best!*

Mrs. Nakamura

A PENDING PURCHASE in downtown Honolulu held confusing questions. Phoning first before going down there seemed best. For my halting inquiry, the person on the phone thought she should consult my previous contact. "With whom did you speak? Was it Mrs. Nakamura or Mrs. Johnson?" That query had no answer from me. After a long delay she came to the phone with the needed information, adding, "And by the way, it was Mrs. Nakamura who helped you."

It brought smiling surprise that my previous encounter contained no thought whatsoever of ethnicity. If only it could be this way for us all the time! My cosmopolitan oyster stresses: *We are all God's children. Think first and foremost of the persons involved and only secondarily, if at all, consider where they came from!*

Dust Rags in Paradise

HON-O-LU-LU was often intoned to stress my utter disbelief of actually *living* in that exquisite place. Then balance would come to mind...there were still dishes, diapers, dust and household duties galore. My Hawaiian oyster taught me: *Life's chores remain, perhaps as payment for the lovely places in which we are privileged to do them!*

Souvenirs Far and Near

LEAVING HONOLULU was going to be difficult. So many treasured memories and "pictures of the heart" had been added to our life pathways. And a precious son had been added to our family. But my husband's Army assignment was now taking him to Vietnam, and returning to be near Pacific Northwest family was my plan for the following year.

My avowed promise shared with friends was that something more than hula lessons would have to be a memento of our Honolulu time! A friend had helped me through early stages of a Hawaiian quilt, the first of two completed in following years. But other kinds of souvenirs remained on my mind in final shopping trips.

Just before our leaving, an attractive accessory caught my eye. It was a dark wood plaque, about two and a half feet in height. On the plaque was mounted half a flower pot, in which was "planted" a sturdy stem holding at its top an arrangement of lush tropical-looking leaves. Sadly the delightful leis never lasted... so this would be a pretty way to have more durable reminder of our Hawaiian interlude.

Well, sort of. Back home in a community near Tacoma, Washington, the plaque was hung in the front hall of my apartment. Its little pot became the niche for reminders to myself about errands, and it was a sure-find place to leave keys.

But one day my keys went on a mysterious journey. My brother-in-law helped me search, including a probe into the greenery of that pot. In so doing he saw the bottom and laughingly asked me, "Hawaiian souvenir? Do you know where this really came from?" He read the embossed company name and its hometown: Tacoma, Washington.

Souvenirs may be purchased anywhere. But the pearl that day from this playful shopping oyster told me: *So many special things in life, both large and small, are likely from far closer to home!*

Doorbells Do Ring!

FIXING COFFEE IN THE KITCHEN while not fully dressed was a past habit. What were my choices if a neighbor or delivery person rang the doorbell? During an enjoyable avocation of touring model homes, my search was for the layout with a route to back bedrooms not passing the front door. Alas, neither our home nor floorplan changed, so it was necessary for me to do so. My modest and cautious oyster taught me this pearl: *Just stay prepared for the unexpected doorbells of life!*

Walter Mitty and Me

"THE SECRET LIFE OF WALTER MITTY" had in its ancient version a scene showing Mitty struggling with grim intensity at the helm of a ship in raging and tempestuous waters.

That was the picture in my mind...almost making me smile...during an extraordinary Northern Virginia storm many years ago. My husband was overseas on Army assignment. My young sons were safe and warm inside. So it was my job to retrieve an extension ladder and figure out how to get it safely and correctly placed for me to clear gutters above the back stairwell. Leaves were badly clogging that area and the downpouring water threatened flooding into the basement.

My clothes were totally drenched, my hair was slathered across my eyes, and the incessant driving rain made seeing anything nearly impossible. But somehow, yes, there was success for Mitty and me.

Two things later became quite clear. (1) What needed to be done was known because previous heavy rain had caused alarming water in our basement family room. We learned where the water would go and how the drain needed to be cleared. So, thankfully, that past storm kept me from sitting this one out.

And (2) this pearl from my drenched oyster: *Needed knowledge and strength will somehow be provided for whatever task is at hand.*

Clouds come floating into my life,
no longer to carry rain or usher storm,
but to add color to my sunset sky.
Rabindranath Tagore

Good Words for LBJ

A TEACHING COLLEAGUE enjoyed sharing with me a history-brushing experience. Her father, a school superintendent, had sought her observations about an applicant who was a college classmate. My friend commented briefly, "Very ambitious and persistent. Very intelligent. He will do well for you, and in anything else he ever decides to do."

A President's career began, my friend believed, because of this conversation. Lyndon Johnson's application was accepted for the teaching position.

My oyster lends a pearl with astute reminder that the powerful and famous travel so many of the same paths we do: *No matter our status, our best efforts and persistence are still required, as life crossroads loom before us.*

Soothing Sooty Feathers

My sons were quite young and we were home alone when some rather confusing, strange noise began. It seemed to come from our fireplace. Momentarily the noise was identified as the sound of a very distressed bird flapping around and battling something or other in our chimney.

Soon it fell with a saddening little thud.

What do we do with an injured bird in our fireplace? How could we help the poor thing? The bird revived just a bit, fluttered its wings, and exited the accident scene. It lighted on a coffee table, on a chandelier, and then on the curtain rod, in apparent fear of those giant beings surrounding him.

One of my boys scurried to open the front door. Sunshine and cool outside air should be inviting after his sooty escapade, but the bird just continued to skitter around our living room hitting things. Despite our gentle direction and emphatic body language, he simply did not want to be steered to freedom out that door.

He did finally go, and languished for some time under bushes in our front yard. Before too long his mother appeared…and off they went. If they were people it could be easily imagined, "But I told you not to…"

"But I just wanted to check it out..." Oh, the stories to tell!

Stories for me, too. Thereafter, thoughts that came to mind involved challenging situations during which sufficient guidance was all around. Caring people were trying to help. An "open door" was ignored as my lame wings faltered and caused me to fall.

My sooty oyster from this fireplace leaves me a pearl: *Accept the help. Follow the guidance. Find that open front door to freedom!*

Special Delivery

ON THE BALL may be apt description for a favorite postal worker from many years ago. He brings smiles to my elder son who recalls playful short mail route interludes. If boys were present in the yard with a ball, our mailman would stop to exchange a few throws and catches before continuing on foot through the rest of our neighborhood. While surely not an expectation from our busy postal people, sharing this tale reminds me of a gentle pearl from my playful oyster: *Even brief moments of spontaneous one-on-one time with a child...my own or someone else's... can create memories that last a lifetime.*

Hidden Tears on the Metro

METROBUS COMMUTING in the Washington, DC area was a long-standing routine for me throughout the 1970s. One particular ride, however, was overshadowed with tearful, gray concerns. A marriage separation was occurring that very day, with confusing factors not yet understood by me even after all these years. An empty house would greet me upon my return home that night. Added to this a business colleague…indeed later to be my husband though that was unknown at the time…was coping with attempted suicide of his estranged wife.

Upon my boarding the bus, our driver's usual smile greeted me. "Good morning! So how are you today?" he asked. Long before, wise ones had taught me that "How are you?" is a greeting rather than an invitation to detail whatever ills prevail at the time.

"Great," was my reply, with perhaps some words added, "…hope you are well today also."

So many smiles around us each day may similarly be covering real problems and needs, for which friendship and prayer should be available when possible. The pearl added that day to my string was from a weeping oyster: *So much turmoil and pain can hover behind the façade of a "good morning" smile; be sensitive for opportunities to make a difference!*

Class B Soap Opera

EARLY MONTHS of our time together in the 1970s brought lengthy hassles with what we tried laughingly to call Class B Soap Opera stuff for my husband and me. Forgoing the ugly details, a brush-across might include detectives following and photographing us, legal and financial challenges, court dates, audits, and embarrassing phone calls to our workplaces.

One evening of literal physical pain, confusion and weeping became a significant time of insight for me. We had received legal papers of yet another pending action and found ourselves in tears and angry words…not raising voices *to* each other, but *with* each other in our shared muddle of feelings. What were we going to do? How in the world would we manage? My chest hurt with stress pain of some kind and my stomach was in knots.

Somehow filtering through all the dark thoughts, insight came like an answer to prayer before we even ventured on that path. There was intense anger and frustration, desire for retribution, gripping resentment and fear. However, what became crystal clear was that all these things in no way touched or affected the perpetrator of the problems. They only affected me.

Forgiveness appeared to be quite a remote possibility, but ongoing time seems to bring that about.

The pearl on my string from this bitter oyster tells me: *While the things others send into my life cannot be controlled, with God's help my reaction to those things can and must be controlled.*

So Soon Old, So Late Smart!

THAT OLD COMEDIAN'S JOKE surely applied to our household finances at times. But we learn!

Cash from a small property sale was coming. Where should it go? A financial guru for whom we did typesetting and graphics shared this firm directive: All extra money should be for investment or savings, rather than regular accounts where it obviously dissipates too speedily. "Extra" is anything beyond employment: refunds, dividends, sales, bonuses, inheritance, gifts, or even a lotto windfall. Yes, we needed to shift gears, without dwelling on past waste or judgment errors.

Indeed a firmer financial foundation is created. Our banking oyster agrees, adding with his pearl another thought: *The wisest plan also puts tithing and regular church and charity gifts high on the ledger.*

Incurable Word Sleuth

FRIENDS OFTEN JOKE that even scanning a restaurant menu for me means proofreading. After years of marriage my husband also got into the game, though he had professed great aversion to grammar in school. One of his favorite finds was, "Select one of our fine wines to compliment your meal." My husband would ask a bemused waiter if they had talking bottles in the wine cellar…how else could they say nice words (compliment) versus going well with something (complement)? Our language indeed has many rocky roads!

My revered journalism teacher stressed correctness no matter what. We were known to have our school paper reprinted if a misspelled name were noted while it was being run. She taught that the importance of fixing an error bears no relationship whatsoever to the number of people who may notice it is wrong.

This got cited often to the office of a particular executive at the Washington, DC retail store where a decade of my career was spent a long while ago. "OK, JoAnne. What did we do now?" that executive would plead. One memorable time it was to note a glaring grammar error heading a sales flyer just mailed to thousands of customers. In it, our store president informed them, "As a valued customer of our store, I invite you to our big sale starting next week." (Ask your son's English teacher!)

Then there was the big poster noticed in our bookstore window one morning. It announced opportunity to meet the author and obtain a signed copy of his book. The book was the second one about the Peter Principle by Laurence Peter. Rather embarrassingly for someone, multiple big signs named him Lawrence Peters.

So my journalism teacher's principle continues to get invoked with this pearl from my proofreading oyster: *Correcting something amiss is surely preferred, no matter who may or may not notice what is wrong!*

They have been at a great feast
of languages and stolen the scraps.
"Shakespeare" Love's Labour's Lost
(And Word Sleuth observation after some editing projects!)

Lazy Dumb

OUR FAMILY LEXICON famously grew when my husband, Bill, defined a "Lazy Dumb" malady. That refers to the careless do-it-later toss which results in a second trip, a separate later chore, or a search for lost items. My efficient oyster echoes Bill and also advises action when something is in my hand the first time: *Just do it now. Be Lazy Smart.*

Sidetrip for a Stranger

CHRISTMAS EVE, and still shopping? By my car at the mall appeared a frightened woman with crumpled note in hand asking in halting English about the closest bus stop.

Following words clarified that her uncertainty was both the stop and which bus to take. Destination? She named a downtown DC hotel and something about being able to get to her embassy from there. Not really too far...why not just take her there? She hesitantly agreed.

Crowded city traffic allowed a bit more time to talk. She was from Egypt and was mystified that someone would spend Christmas Eve time helping a stranger from far away. With tearful eyes she took my hand upon taking leave saying simply, "Your kindness will be remembered. What are your words? Merry Christmas."

My ride-sharing oyster here firmly reminds me: *Thoughtfulness extended at any time, both to friend and stranger, may travel in far paths unknown to us. Do it anyway!*

It is when you give of yourself
that you truly give.
Kahlil Gibran, The Prophet

Dip and Carve

DIP AND CARVE CANDLES were an intriguing avocation for me for a few long ago years. It was an art learned through extraordinarily gifted nephews who took their talent and the lovely results of it to many locations here and abroad. Mine were taken only to fairs and art shows in Florida.

Our home at the time was perfect for this venture. An outdoor atrium area was great for setting up my wax supplies, dipping vats, carving table and drying rack. A tree growing through the roof there and an adjacent rock arrangement with bubbling, falling water added to the pleasant surroundings. Turn on soft radio music and many hours of work could proceed beautifully well.

My big disappointment from this era was that the timing of our move from that home, and the accompanying necessity of suspending the candle venture, caused me to have virtually no evidence of my lovely work. All but a couple or three of my candles had been sold, with the assumption that the coming fall season and later holidays approaching would bring many more. That never happened.

Often my introspective moments bring the memories, and the insights. Perhaps it could be said that our God molds our lives in similar fashion. We are dipped into this experience and then that one. We are formed and carved by a Master Artisan. The tools may sometimes hurt. They twist and turn, cut excess away, and then form a unique creation.

My candle oyster, indeed dripping colorful wax, lends this pearl for my string: *Simply trust that Master Artisan. Whatever "dipping and carving" is necessary will bring His intended and beautiful design for our lives.*

The TV with Eternal Life

MY TV IS OLDER than most techs who have ever had brushing contact. There has been cable hookup and such procedures, but never has a single dollar been spent on the set itself. Mitsubishi is now into all the most stellar modern electronic features, defined only with my grandsons' help. But what excuse can be made for that purchase yet, when my old set just will not die? Eternal life, to be sure!

My wise shopping oyster must have watched over us in this early 1980s decision. Despite it being a time of difficult financial challenge we did act upon, and have since proved, his pearl of wisdom: *Seeking and choosing best quality will in the long run be the most money-saving purchase.*

Pretty Things

"SOME THINGS IN LIFE are worth getting fussy about, but this is not one of them!" My sons used to hear this often from me upon some kitchen or household mishap.

"Well then, what is?" challenged my older son once after my repeated admonition. Perhaps he was considering a fallen photograph, a broken toy, or the accidentally cracked dish he was holding. But my patience comes through a long family line.

At the time it was tempting to refer to our extensive shelf of Czechoslovakian crystal as "worth getting fussy about". A wiser thought prevailed. Why have all those pretty things if they never get used for fear of some damage? Why indeed? They are just things after all, and can usually be replaced.

Living by that premise today, both ice cream and after dinner drinks may be enjoyed using those mid-century crystal pieces. Breakfast cereal goes into a Spode Jewel bowl, or omelets and mixed fruit go onto Wedgwood luncheon pieces. A treasured spoon collection of 110-year-old sterling resides in an equally antique container on my counter, with constant use. Extensive arrays of lovely Westmoreland depression glass and Wade Irish porcelain throughout my home hold everything from mints and personal toiletries to flowers, tea, coffee pods or lunch. An 18th-century Sheffield silver tray and basket hold my kitchen towels.

When grandchildren visit, remembering where "regular stuff" is stashed is not even that important. These things are enjoyed in my home, after all, because prior owners chose to put them in a display case and use them only rarely or never.

Introspective times cause me to add to my crystal and antique collections all the other beauty enfolding me daily. Lush tropical flowers. The leaves. Sunshine through the boughs. Moonlight peeking around the clouds. Lovely fresh new ferns appearing after extensive rain. Palms swaying in the wind. God smiles and adds scampering squirrels and colorful birds to all this...daily enjoyed by me while bike riding or just sipping from one of those special collectibles in my Florida room.

The pearl from my antique oyster is simple: *Enjoy all the pretty things. Treasure them. Use and share them. Give thanks for them!*

I can no other answer make but thanks,
and thanks, and ever thanks.

"Shakespeare" Twelfth Night

Small World Indeed

A FAVORITE "SMALL WORLD" JOURNEY was launched as my Orlando dentist noted a troubling anomaly during an otherwise routine checkup. Instructing prompt follow-up, he presented a card for his recommended specialist.

The name on that card seemed so familiar. Could it possibly be...?

In that specialist's office soon thereafter, my recently changed name clouded his recognition of a former patient and Army post neighbor. So it was an unbelievably rare experience to warn him as he scanned my films, "Do not be too critical of that work. You did it!"

Bottom line, this was the picture: 1960s to 1980s in time. Honolulu to Orlando in distance. Same dentist to correct the same tooth. Small world indeed!

My dental oyster reminded me: *Past times and far people are all much closer than we think. If nothing else, they bring great stories to share!*

I feel like a fugitive from the law of averages!

Cartoon caption from a 1944 issue of "Up Front"

Charlie Brown Leaves

RAKING LEAVES was not a favorite task for my husband, Bill, but he did it so well. Our very ordinary suburban yard does have, amazingly, over 80 trees in or surrounding it. Constantly in all seasons, something is falling from those trees! Time, tools, yard bags and patience are all required.

So many times in my recollection, Bill would be standing in the yard with rake in hand, and a dozen or more bulging yard waste bags in rows by the fence. With a blower he had cleared the driveway, to go with the neatly raked yard. But soon a wisp of breeze would flutter through. Then Bill would look up with a Charlie Brown shrug and watch, as a few more leaves wafted down onto the cleaned areas.

Remembering a favorite old cartoon, his resigned response was, "God always gets the last word!"

The raking and the driveway-clearing tasks are now mine, and smiling memories do balance busy times in the yard. Indeed those old words extend themselves into other areas of my life as that wisdom is internalized for me. Whether it is rain or leaves falling into my yard, or dilemmas and challenges falling into my life, it is vital prayerfully to remember the pearl on my string from this very busy oyster: *Listen well for God does, indeed, get the last word!*

Great Shopping Coups

WHILE MY MENTAL SHOPPING LIST had notes of basement storeroom shelving, a simple answer appeared in my employer's warehouse. Research job duties for a major Washington, DC retailer took me often between there and my city office. Shopping in both places of course happened.

What was noted this particular day was a sizeable array of pressed board stuff which could be for entertainment centers, book shelves…or yes, basement storage units. Asked about pricing and such, a nearby worker promised to consult his manager. As the items appeared to be customer returns, a quite low price might have been expected, but surely not as low as later learned. The worker reported to me that his impatient manager simply wanted to get rid of the stuff. Immediately. "Tell Jo Anne she can have the whole batch for a buck!"

That was several just-right shelving units used in multiple homes for decades. The receipt should be framed and mounted, for with my employee discount they cost eighty cents!

ANOTHER SURPRISE BARGAIN was exquisite stemware offered at an estate sale. Sharing them with family was the plan, for our crystal cabinets were already full. The price was simply too good to pass up.

The sale manager quietly reminded us of the half-price arrangement scheduled for that afternoon. Then she confided, "They are lovely. But of course you know they are not real."

"But they look so much like the ones we already have. They will be nice regardless," was my uncertain response. The 40 pieces were carefully packed for us right at the half-price time.

A couple items needed very minor touch-up by my crystal genie who had performed miracles before. He asked, "Do you know what you have here? Despite what you were told, these *are* hand-blown, hand-cut crystal. You seem to have paid for the 40 pieces less than the value of two of them!"

SALE? WELL NO, AND YES! Remembering this purchase brings smiles. During my careful scrutiny of new issues in a series of collectible Christmas ornaments a nearby shopper observed, "Oh, those are so expensive. You will probably find them on sale if you travel a bit. She named a store in a city the rest of the way across Florida. It seemed worth the journey.

In that store later the manager conveyed confusing news. "No, those are not included in our sale today.

However, I can give them to you for half price." Despite his strange reasoning, it was an offer better than the "sale" price and surely not to be refused!

My shopping oyster reminds me of this pearl: *Just be vigilant. Needs and desires are met in such unexpected ways…even on a slim budget!*

Mow it all Down?

A YARD WORKER was at my home to help with a few tasks beyond my tools or ability. Under a huge tree in one corner of my yard is a constant growth of sturdy tall sprigs promising an undesired full forest at some future time. Before heading to work there were only brief minutes to outline my requests…the main one involving thinning out that growth under the tree. Upon my return home that evening, it was quite disappointing to learn the worker's interpretation of "thinning"; it included a complete close-crop mowing of the big spread of border grass. That took many seasons to regrow.

My pearl from this yard toiling oyster was simply this: *Ensure understanding with very specific requests or instructions, lest unexpected results come!*

A Cash Stash

IN FLORIDA we are constantly advised about preparations and stock-up items for a hurricane or any power outage emergency. Reasons vary but all parts of our country have similar challenges at differing times. One detail seldom mentioned is cash. If ATMs do not work, how would most people survive these days?

So a cash stash was on the list for my husband and me as one storm approached. Then it seemed wise simply to leave the money in its secret place...out of sight, out of mind so to speak, so it does not get used for coffee shop or bookstore jaunts. One time later it was oh, so appreciated as an extended family visit up north loomed with miniscule notice. With laughably brief time to get myself, my wardrobe, my car and my home in order...getting to the bank was not one of the needed chores.

Whether for a death in the family, a surprise journey, a natural or manmade emergency of some kind...my financial guru oyster counsels simply: *Plastic is not always possible or advisable. Maintain a cash stash for the unexpected!*

The wise look ahead to see what is coming.
Proverbs 14:7 NLT

The Pla$tic Trap

MANY YEARS IN RETAIL employment brought valuable lessons, some learned or acted upon perhaps a bit late.

With early family life and all the attendant furnishing requirements, children's clothing and various ongoing household needs, it was ever so great...it seemed at the time...to have advantage of an employee discount. Just pull out my card, sign the sales slip designed by me in an upstairs office, and plan on periodic payment of that bill. Paying monthly minimum... sadly a common trap...seemed so easy.

However, paying those minimums ran up an unwise amount of debt for us, particularly in later time when a new household was being established. It took such a very long while to be extricated from that debt. (One of my current obligations under $2,000 indicates that with only minimum payments it will be paid off in 13 years, at a cost of nearly $6,000!) Soon wiser math began to prevail. Since then, on my own now, my cards are used for convenience but paid in full each month.

That policy used to seem impossible but my very calculating oyster taught me about this vital pearl: *If it is not affordable for me today in cash, it will surely not be affordable next month and thereafter with 22% or more interest added!*

Anonymous Ancestors

THE TALE SHARED HERE is just one of many from intense genealogy research during years of creating family history albums for each of my sons. Many photographs acquired were quite confusing. One in particular looked like the kind of snapshot taken behind a home after a big holiday dinner. It was mounted on a small card as late-1800s style often dictated. As it was not marked in any way, my sisters were opting for just discarding it.

At my insistence they did keep it, and it was added to my research tasks. Obvious things were noted. My maternal grandparents were quite definitely there, and great grandparents were recognized from other photographs. A woman in white appeared to be a bride. *Who were all those people?* After long research, including finding some distant cousins on the internet, the truth formed. My grandparents and a brother (next to the woman in white) were married in a double ceremony in their Dakota Territory home in 1888. This was three generations of extended family and clergymen at that home. The only known memento of my grandparents' marriage came so close to being discarded simply because it lacked markings.

The grandfather in this picture was involved in another huge search. We had a portrait of five handsome men. One appeared to be my grandfather perhaps at college age in the 1870s, but it was from an Illinois studio while we knew only of his birth in New York. Long searches. Many letters. Census hunts. Document acquisition. Professional researchers. Bottom line: Grandpa's family had moved from New York to Illinois. We eventually identified 12 of them. His father died in a cholera epidemic. His mother, whose picture was later shared from another distant relative "found" online, lived until the 1890s. We learned of her strong faith, testimony of which clearly shined in final moments of her life.

We treasure these photographs and the stories learned about a few of our precious ancestors. However, so very much work, study and expense was caused simply because the pictures were not identified.

Full names, dates, and place should be on all pictures, especially portraits. (William, two years, does not say enough! William who? Two years when?) Grandchildren will appreciate it, and further descendants will not have so many anonymous ancestors. My "soapbox" instruction for so many now is this wisdom from my very persistent genealogy oyster: *Just mark or clearly tag all those pictures!*

I will note you in my book of memory.

"Shakespeare" King Henry VI

Another Day, Another Journey

LIFE BLESSINGS SUCH AS TRAVEL can involve unexpected wisdom. My husband, Bill, often expressed impatience with the apparent desire of so many to see and do everything. Now. This week. We are here, so let us do it all while there is a chance. This is an unrealistic manifesto of the soon-to-be-disappointed traveler.

Wherever we were…on business, family visit, choir tour, or pleasure…Bill opted for a more leisurely pace. If not, he maintained, it would be true that not only would we not see and do everything, we would in our haste not really enjoy the things we *did* see and do. Like "Disney in a Day" we found so many places we traveled to be equally impossible to traverse and do any justice at all to available opportunities with only brief time on our schedule.

Vienna, Prague or the Normandy Beach areas were delightful challenges for us. And later trips of mine included uncountable delights in several other European areas accented with exquisite cruises on the Thames, the Seine and the Rhine. All this brought the same wisdom to bear.

My oyster with the crumpled and crowded passport echoes my late husband in this valuable pearl:

Save some plans for another day, another journey; if not, weariness and impatience will make me unable to enjoy THIS day and THIS journey.

One by one the sands are flowing,
One by one the moments fall;
Some are coming, some are going;
Do not try to grasp them all.
Adelaide Procter

Pain vs Gain

DURING A BOUT WITH MYSTERIOUS and persistent back pain, opportunity came for sessions with two different massage therapists. One was a pleasant interlude, perhaps similar to a spa visit on a cruise. The second one was quite different, instead adding to my significant pain. This therapist seemed to find and firmly manipulate every hurting spot, as she worked her way across shoulders and down my back. The welcome great results far outweighed my temporarily raised discomfort level.

My chiropractic oyster reminded me of a needed pearl, also famously cited by Adlai Stevensen: *Without pains there are no gains!*

Mystery Ingredients

A FAVORITE CINNAMON ROLL recipe came out of long obscurity in my formerly very busy kitchen. They were to be for between-service breakfast munchies for our choir the next morning, and making them again was a welcome, familiar task.

All went well, and my added plus was the discipline of not constantly tasting the concoction as my former bad habit had been. Well, almost successful there. In the very last step of rolling out the dough a stray chunk did find its way into my mouth. It was ever so fortunate that that happened, for it tasted terribly strong in some way. What in the world was my big mistake? These same rolls have been casting wonderful aroma in my kitchen for 40 years or more.

As finally analyzed, there are just too many white things in my baking cupboard. All are in similar airtight stacking containers rather than their original boxes or bags, a necessary habit in Florida climate. There is flour, self-rising flour, corn starch, protein powder, dry milk, stevia, powdered sugar, regular sugar in two sizes of containers, and salt in a container similar to one of the sugars. So it appeared that instead of sugar in the dough, one third cup of salt had been added instead!

Fortunately just the story was shared with choir friends the next day, rather than those salty rolls. While the second batch was rising, a long-delayed process of labeling all those containers was tackled. . .and the salt and sugar were tasted, to prevent any future errors!

Besides the newly-extended duties of a labeling machine, the pearl gleaned from this salty oyster in my kitchen says: *Familiar processes do not ensure success. It is wise to double check and use care, even in the most common tasks!*

A Bit of Salt!

WHIPPING CREAM for a planned dessert treat was my task, seemingly so routine. Childhood memories of cream from the milk of our own cow seemed ancient as powdered and aerosol products came into use. The old way was chosen, but somehow was not going quite right and lumpiness began to form. My husband appeared and after quick appraisal advised with a smile, "Just add a bit of salt to that and you will have some good butter!"

My oyster left this simple pearl: *The old way may be good, but maintain a few delicious "Plan B" options if it does not go well!*

Once in a Lifetime Cookies

MAKING NAPOLEONS seemed a delicious plan in an early, more adventuresome phase of my cooking career. A full afternoon was spent following instructions. Mix carefully. Roll out, brush with butter and fold. Freeze. Roll out and fold again. Then again. And again. When completed they tasted fine. However, their final appearance just did not meet my idea of the perfect treat to share at an approaching wives' coffee gathering on the Army post where we lived. A new plan for me meant enrolling the blender. My Napoleons became crumbs.

After assessing the amount of flour and butter already used, a bundt cake recipe was found and adapted. To the Napoleon crumbs were added the second recipe's ingredients...and out came the most delectable coffeecake ever to dwell in my kitchen. Coffee party attendees asked for my recipe. All they could be told was, "Making this great treat starts with being a flop at making Napoleons!"

This plan lives still, with a special freezer box labeled "Once in a Lifetime Mix". Into that box go crumbs of anything that is not quite right...maybe a bit too brown, maybe broken when removed from the cookie sheet. Then there is a continuing trail...too many nuts chopped for coating favorite treats, too much streusel mixed, more shaved chocolate than those brownies needed, crumbles from the bottom of the s'mores mix bag. This is truly a waste-not plan!

Then when treats are needed for Writers' Club friends or between-service snacks for the choir, a little of this mix is appropriated. Some butter and egg is added, and whatever flavoring inspires me that day. Cookies can be baked as is, or balled up, chilled and then rolled in more of the "Once in a Lifetime" crumbs. Sometimes melted chocolate poured over a bowlful creates a tempting cross between a brownie and fudge. Always delicious...but never is a recipe available to share!

This is surely a life analogy sermon in my kitchen! Adding this pearl to my string comes accompanied by a song heard often on our local gospel station. (And God says)
I'm gonna turn it into something different.
I'm gonna turn it into something good.
I'm gonna take all the broken pieces
and make something beautiful like only I could.
(excerpt from Something Beautiful by Steven Curtis Chapman).

He that is of a merry heart hath a continual feast.
Proverbs 15:15 KJV

Right Place, Right Time

OUR CHURCH CHOIR was invited to sing at a nearby community college. It was not quite like a concert in Vienna or Prague, but there had been a CD audition and our taking part that day was an honor.

The occasion was a gathering of church and school music leaders from all of Florida. Our "chance drawing" of singing order put us at the end, and many weary participants had chosen already to leave. Despite many hours of rehearsal time perfecting our director's selections, it was so disappointing that those remaining to hear us barely outnumbered our singers. It was tempting to wonder why we were even there.

Before long an answer came. While chatting with some dear choir friends outside the auditorium we were approached with hearty greetings from another couple. They were introduced to me as friends and "music buddies" from former South Florida choral activities. These old friends, it turned out, were planning to lead an extended European music tour. Would we like to join the group?

Would we? Well, yes, of course! Though we had traveled to Europe before, this tour was indeed unlike any other. There were different people and places, and different challenges, such as memorizing the entire repertoire. Our time was filled to overflowing with precious once-in-a-lifetime experiences. A singular "angel moment" encountered was shared in my book *My Leis upon the Water.* Our full itinerary through London, Paris, Lake Geneva villages, Rothenburg, Venice and all points between could merit an entire additional book. So many "pictures of the heart" were acquired, as well as an abundance of the traditional kind.

And, yes, it all came about because of a concert that had caused questions of why we were there. Was this just "right place, right time" coincidence or accident?

A talented singing oyster added a pearl to my string after this chapter of my life: *Right place, right time is wherever we are. God does have plans for us which just may not be so apparent right away!*

Oh Lord that lends me life,
lend me a heart replete with thankfulness.
"Shakespeare" King Henry VI

O sing unto the Lord a new song.
Psalm 96:1 KJV

Tree Rain

WHEN AN EARLY MORNING WALK was in my routine, before-dawn darkness sometimes made evaluating the weather challenging. After a check outside our front door, the sound of rain could alter my plans.

When the truth finally came to me, it was intriguing to learn how deceptive had been a simple sound in the darkness. After nighttime rain, it would continue for a long while to *sound* as if it were still raining as wetness dropped from leaf to leaf on the trees. We came to call this *tree rain.* So often it had wrongly kept me in!

This discovery seemed to fit other situations. How often does incomplete or misleading information keep us from doing something? Members of our choir commonly overhear comments to the effect of, "I would enjoy singing with a group like that. But they must all be professionals. I would never pass the auditions." A few professionals, yes, but we are also blessed with a superb director who has unmatched gifts for bringing out the best in all of us.

What about a writing group? "They must all be published authors. What could I contribute?" With all experience levels represented, just the sharing is beneficial for everyone. And making new friends is great, too.

What about a continuing ed class? "After so long, I could not hack all that study and test stuff now. A grandma in their midst would bring snickers." After such a class once, evaluation told me that with my experience and expertise *teaching* the group would have been rather routine, with no need to have worried about doing well as a student.

For years certain opportunities to go abroad were not pursued because of vague feeling that one should "learn the language" to travel safely or get much out of it. Overcoming this, seven European jaunts, mostly singing tours, have been logged on my passport.

It is common to have situations such as these where faulty information or our own false assumptions prevent us from venturing on a rewarding path. The pearl on my string from this well-soaked oyster: *Do not let the tree rain keep you in!*

Intelligent people are always open to new ideas.
In fact, they look for them.
Proverbs 18:15 NLT

To everything there is a season,
and a time to every purpose under the heaven.
Ecclesiastes 3:1 KJV

Evicting My Pet Peeves

PET PEEVE. From where in the world did that term ever come? Are there regular peeves, and only the most perverse ones are pets? If we "feed" them do they stick around longer, as do the other well-cared-for pets in our homes?

It is bothersome when thoughts on such matters divert me from more productive pursuits. My pet peeves are diverse to be sure. They range from errant apostrophes or certain ignorantly misused words, to the fitness guru who does lunges and varying stretches from block to block on her daily outings while so rarely interrupting her routine for a simple wave, nod, or "good morning" greeting.

Sometimes fostering a peeve can trouble me for blocks after a driver ignores my polite attempt to let him enter the traffic stream. Or one can bother me all the way to my car after experiencing the shopper who has waited for several minutes in line and several minutes for checkout, and THEN decides to fumble around for payment. Perhaps my most pervasive peeve is telephone and computer spam. On and on they go. Those peeves need to go somewhere!

My oyster when irked tries poetry from time to time:

My peeves need not occupy
So very much of my mind.
Surely there is a wiser plan
For me to finally find.
Oh yes, here is what
I really need to do...
Just send my Pet Peeves off
To God's faraway zoo!

Just Look Up

A PROLIFIC AMOUNT of nature was changing location in my yard, causing dozens of huge leaf bags to be generated over many days. With a rake still in my hand it seemed this situation would have no end, though it did bring welcome fresh air breaks. Something dropped, causing me to look up. My chagrin with what was there almost brought laughter. The huge tree arching above was full of fresh leaves of the new season. Did it happen overnight? Somehow that was totally missed by me because my focus had been so firmly on the task with what was under my feet.

My leafy oyster winked, leaving his pearl: *Remember to look up! See future seasons of life rather than simply raking debris from past ones!*

Right Either Way!

WE ARE WHAT WE EAT is a health maxim in popular circulation. More seriously, we are what we think. Sadly that can start with what a child hears. My Father memorably observed, "You will probably have a weight problem your whole life."

That did indeed turn out to be true for a long while… because he said so, after all. Later defining my own weight issues and goals seemed wiser, with doctors giving me a differing basis of thought.

Too often are young ones introduced, "He is our mischievous one," or "She is my shy one." Those children grow up believing whatever they keep hearing about themselves…as have we.

Awareness of positive words and their power was a welcomed outcome of some past seminar sessions. Rather than "We cannot afford that," affirm "That can be in our budget another time." Instead of "I am just no good at numbers," or name any subject, think instead, "Challenge, yes, and there are new things for me to learn." In daily talk to others, "Remember to do…" is far better reminder than, "Do not forget…"

The principle is: Whether we say we can or cannot do something, we are right either way! Whatever we keep telling ourselves will play out as truth in our lives, for good or for ill.

My oyster guru has read Norman Vincent Peale and reminds me of this pearl: *Choose the positive thoughts and words to tell myself, in order to create the positive results in my life!*

Parkmarks

LIKE BOOKMARKS, PARKMARKS may be good insurance for me. We used to joke that it was my husband's job to remember where we parked, so that detail seldom even entered my thoughts. He has been gone many years now and still come so many times of "Where in the world is the car?" One memorable family experience underlined this dangerous slight. On a "sisters trip" in Southern California we returned to the parking lot after a few hours indoors. It was amusing to realize that none of the four of us remembered where we parked. Not only that… because it was a rental, we were not even sure what our car looked like!

My parking oyster turns more serious to counsel that life's roadways, or stopping points thereon, are rarely marked "Mickey" or "Donald" as at Disney. *Wise searching and firm orientation are needed to clarify both my present and future goals.*

Seeking Real Connection

IN TODAY'S WORLD connectedness appears to be the desired norm for every moment of living. A distinction needs to be firm about REAL connection versus the electronic kind. The scenario shared here has been so haunting to me; my prayer surely is that guilt of such consummate thoughtlessness will never be mine.

The scene was a local surgery center, where some rather routine correction for a troublesome foot issue was scheduled by my doctor. Anesthesia and the various steps involved were not exactly exciting to contemplate, but my experience said to trust the professionals.

On a gurney across from me in the pre-op waiting area was a very young boy who appeared perhaps to have had a sports injury of some kind on his leg. While he was being prepared for anesthesia hookup his father was on a cell phone…very distinctly business, not personal. He checked in at his office. He called a client. He checked back with his office, then called another client, and then another. Perhaps the equipment was hampering his thinking, so he stepped away for yet another call.

When the medical technician returned to check on the boy, she apparently sensed a troubled aura, and softly asked if he had any questions.

"It does not hurt now," he replied tearfully, "...but could I die?"

My tears flowed. It was unbelievable to me that that man could so flagrantly flaunt his perceived indispensability at his job, while utterly missing awareness of his nearby son who was in sad fear of the unknown, thinking he might die.

Modern wireless wonders may snarl us into traps of dependence and sometimes keep us from cultivating real God-given bond with those around us. There should be friendly smiles, hugs, comforting arms on a shoulder, listening ears and heart available in someone else's need, or quiet prayer for a family member or friend.

Electronic stuff? Only maybe. The pearl added to my string from this sad oyster whispered to me: *Plug first and foremost into God's firm and real connection!*

If I can stop one heart from breaking
I shall not live in vain;
If I can ease one life the aching,
or cool one pain,
Or help one fainting robin
unto his nest again,
I shall not live in vain.
Emily Dickinson

Tiffany's Ghost

TIFFANY INVADED OUR LIVES AND HEARTS, holding them firmly for many years. She adopted me before we adopted her, meeting me during my daily bike rides, seeking friendly attention. She was an exquisite kitten, all white with very long and soft fur. Upon learning Tiffany was an abandoned stray about to be taken by animal control to mollify complaining neighbors, we rescued her.

Through the years Tiffany blessed us with her tender presence. She was loving and friendly in every way but just not as much of a "lap cat" as may have been preferred. She rarely shared our bed except to pounce upon it to announce breakfast time. But somehow... how did she know?...she found her way to the pillow at my shoulder and purred me to sleep on the day my husband had died. That became her new sleeping place. She was a precious comfort for a few more years, until her own death in my arms on another very sad day.

Throughout Tiffany's time with us her fur was a constant challenge. Everywhere. Clothes. Furniture. Drapes. Carpet. Windowsills. Her fur trails even increased through her last months of illness. After her death...a long while after...her fur was still found around my home. When cleaning required rare moving of a heavy piece of furniture, evidence of Tiffany's past presence there brought smiles.

Last traces of my beloved pet were not to be parted with. Some of those cleaning finds reside on my family room bookshelf in a tiny jar labeled "Tiffany's Ghost".

This was like finding old toys after the children are grown, or clearing a cluttered desk after a loved one is gone. The pearl added to my string from this vacuuming oyster told me: *New perspective can create welcome treasure out of former problems or challenges.*

PS: Sometimes comes contemplation of my own "fur" so to speak. It is scattered over uncounted photographs, writings, mementos, research files, letters and a lifetime of personal and family keepsakes. Hopefully these traces of mine left behind will be treasured also, like Tiffany's!

Untimely Buy

CAPTIVATING INDIAN CHILDREN as seen by beloved artist Ted DeGrazia in turn captivated me. We found the plate collection late, when first issue was $250 up from $35. Okay, bypass that one but go on with the others. After slated issuing years we had all but that first one. It then came for a never-to-be-admitted price. My collectible oyster reminds me: *If it is at all in my realm of reality, buy it the first time!*

Just Do It!

FENCES MAKE GOOD NEIGHBORS is an old adage, but perhaps not always true. In my daily habit of simply gathering tree debris that has fallen in the night, it has not occurred to me to define position of the lot line in my side yard. No fence is there. While at my chore time anyway, just picking it up and helping my neighbor a bit seems to be a better plan.

For a long while near my home there languished a stash appearing to be remnants of a demolished tile job, becoming one of those pet peeves shared in a previous tale. Neither the homeowner nor a variety of county workers adopted rsponsibility. Such a silly task perhaps, but it did become mine. A few pieces went into my pockets on each bike ride along that stretch, and home they went into my trash. Yes, an extremely long process…but the tiles are gone and that area is now clear again with thriving grass and a few wild flowers.

Often it is easy to question "whose job it is" to pick it up, or fix it up, or clean it up. There are no fences here. Any such task can be thoughtfully adopted.

The instructive pearl for me from this rake-toting oyster: *Waste no time defining a fence or lot line. Just do it!*

Pathways from Chillon

THE CASTLE AT CHILLON on the shores of Lake Geneva in Switzerland was only one of so many beautiful and historic highlights of our singing tour.

It was indeed hard to absorb just being in a place where nearly a millennium of human experiences have occurred involving royal residents, warriors and prisoners. Being down in the dim prison area and looking through bars to the lake did bring regret about my lax literature study regarding Lord Byron. A book with his famous poem telling the story of the *Prisoner of Chillon* was a definite must-purchase before leaving.

Then came a choice. The bus was going next to Montreux, farther up the lake shore. The more adventuresome among us chose instead to walk the pathway. That span from Chillon to Montreux was among the most memorable "picture of the heart" walks of my life. Photos of the regular kind could do no justice whatsoever to the atmosphere, the feeling, the peacefulness, the tranquil beauty.

My alpine hiking oyster left me his lovely pearl: *The convenient and the fast way to get there will most probably be a dim second to simply walking the path and savoring the journey a bit more.*

God Ain't Through with Me Yet!

A RECENT AND LONG-AWAITED knee surgery experience gave me a great deal of new perspective. My health history has always seemed rather boring, while obviously being one of my life's great blessings. It brought smiles to tell multiple clipboard-toting questioners about my near-50s son causing my last hospital stay.

But throughout that span barely speckled with only an occasional cold or bronchial distress, my habits got very lax regarding asking questions beyond "With or without food?" for sparse medication needs. Danger loomed.

A few weeks after my surgery, a particular medication was strengthened and refilled, contrary to intent of the original prescriber. Then, directions for the needed monitoring of its effect on my blood were unclear or absent. Because no anomaly was apparent right away, my usual no-questions habit persisted. Oh, the lessons to be learned!

A little later serious and profuse internal bleeding occurred. A Sunday morning phone consultation told me it was probably just routine infection and added medication was called to my pharmacy. However, Monday follow-up on that brought a scary new path, an immediate trip to the Emergency Room. Besides the persistent, excruciating pain, uppermost in my awareness during the following several days was repeating comment of various professionals about the critical timing. Any more delay in my getting there could have been fatal.

Despite firm faith in later new life, being brushed so closely with a possible end to this one was sobering indeed! In my quest for meaning to it all the strains of *It is Well with my Soul* stirred right along with an old comedian's proclamation, "God ain't through with me yet!" My AAA pearl gleaned from this very critically ill oyster: *Assume nothing. Ask questions. Acquire firm understanding of what is going on, when issues of health and life are at stake.*

PS: My heart generally seeks the rainbow arching over gray times. Could there possibly be one here? Of course! During weeks of enforced non-activity, many tales long wafting through my mind developed into these stories here shared. So my life-and-death questions did have a rainbow, hopefully bringing smiles and blessing to readers of *My String of Pearls.*

...verses of wisdom as a necklace of pearls
on strands of my love.
Kahlil Gibran, A Tear and a Smile

Unstrung Pearls

A FEW "PS" WORDS from the author...sort of like sticky notes remaining as writing lulls!

BESIDES MY FAMILY of course figuring into stories here shared...indeed they suggested some of them... it was delightful to bring two of my grandsons into this project. The ethereal cover background, accenting the pearls just right, came from a creation of Alex and Griffin Kinkade. Lots of their stuff is on my fridge, but their Grandma found an even nicer use for a unique piece of art they presented at Christmas. You are very special, guys!

MY STRING OF PEARLS and all the strange but helpful oysters in playful analogy therein will hopefully bring smiles and inspiration to readers. My intention is to donate proceeds to my church or a choir project, so do recommend this book to a lot of friends! Then help the effort even more by going to Amazon.com and leaving comments. My thanks!

A SPECIAL THANK YOU to Kathy Schubitz for her patience and professionalism throughout the preparation of this book. We comment often that readers, while enjoying the written words and design appeal, cannot fathom all that it takes to bring them about! But Kathy knows...and does it all so well!

"SHAKESPEARE" appears in quotation marks with any cited lines for reasons explained in *My Leis upon the Water.* This authorship issue has been a lifelong study with books being continually added to my library. Friends will warn: *Do not get her started!* For me it still boils down to that insurmountable offering of simple human reason: The most towering intellect ever to weave such priceless and profound trails through our language would not leave illiterate family. And perhaps he may possess at least one book, or be able to spell and write his own name. Save this for a chat over coffee sometime!

CHALLENGE from the Word Sleuth! A writing awareness dating from my Whitworth University years has been extended into *My String of Pearls.* It was confusing that no readers outside of family correctly identified the composition effort when it appeared in my previous book. A few classmates did offer answers...but not the intended one.

My challenge involves a rather rare feat of text editing which produces more relatable words, in one realm of writing theory. What very common factor is missing? Be the first to find the answer!

Previous Pearls

My Leis upon the Water
also by Jo Anne French
goes so well with
My String of Pearls
in any reading collection!
It is a similar gathering
of pearls of inspiration,
beauty, humor and love.
A few favorites were adapted
and shared in both books.

Published in 2011
by RPJ Legacy Books.
Available at Amazon.com
or by order from
a local bookstore.

Both make great gifts!
Contact the author to receive
an autographed copy.

Gleaner of these Gems

JO ANNE FRENCH confesses to a lifelong love affair with our language. Her many pathways have honed extensive skills in editing, newswriting, typesetting, publishing, printing, business forms design and graphic arts. Yes, fingers always in the ink, as esteemed 1950s high school and Whitworth University mentors foresaw.

Tales about the erudite "oysters" introduced in playful analogy in this book reveal a full and memorable swath from Jo Anne's girlhood in Seattle, Washington to widowhood years near Orlando, Florida. Along her roadway she was a teacher, sales trainer, systems analyst and "Word Sleuth" in diverse settings. European trips, mostly singing tours, added even more to the experiences drawn upon by those wise oysters. They bestowed significant insight involving both smiles and challenge, all recounted here in *My String of Pearls.*

Jo Anne is an avid reader and crossword addict. She is also a confirmed chocoholic baker, but only when sharing with choir or Writers' Club friends brings excuse, she maintains. Other avocations are related in some of the pearl stories...bringing ideas already wafting through her mind for yet another book. Watch for it!

Parting Pearls

ROUND AND PERFECT
does not define every pearl,
as designs used in this book show.
They are in many forms and shades.
Some may smile upon learning
there are even chocolate pearls…
not edible, just of pretty dark hue.

PEARLS COME FROM PAIN,
most pertinent to the point
of many stories here shared.
A grain of sand gives irritation
to the oyster and in defense
it then forms a lovely gem.
The ultimate life lesson
from these wise oysters!

www.ingramcontent.com/pod-product-compliance
Lightning Source LLC
LaVergne TN
LVHW051155080426
835508LV00021B/2645